I Love Football

Hunter Davies was born in Renfrew in 1936. He has written more than 40 books and, as a journalist, he contributes to the *Sunday Times* and writes a weekly football column in the *New Statesman*. He is an avid collector of football memorabilia. He lives with his wife in the Lake District and in London.

And, in case you were wondering, that's not him on page 1 . . .

Previous books by Hunter Davies include:

The Beatles: the Authorised Biography
The Glory Game
The Fan
Boots, Balls and Haircuts
Dwight Yorke: the Official Biography
Gazza: My Story (with Paul Gascoigne)
The Eddie Stobart Story

I Love Football

A Match Made in Heaven

Hunter Davies

headline

First published in 2006
by HEADLINE BOOK PUBLISHING

1

ISBN 0 7553 1470 0

Typeset by SX Composing DTP, Rayleigh, Essex
Printed and bound in Great Britain by Clays Ltd, St Ives plc

Headline's policy is to use papers that are natural, renewable and
recyclable products and made from wood grown in sustainable forests.
The logging and manufacturing processes are expected to conform to
the environmental regulations of the country of origin.

HEADLINE BOOK PUBLISHING
A division of Hodder Headline
338 Euston Road
London NW1 3BH

www.headline.co.uk
www.hodderheadline.com

Illustrations courtesy of the author, with thanks to the Football
Postcard Collectors Club (p. 12); and Stuart Clarke,
www.homesoffootball.co.uk (p. 83).

CONTENTS

CHAPTER ONE

Why Football Fans Follow Football Teams

H. DAVIES

MOST PEOPLE HAVE a favourite team. Whether they are old or young, male or female, big or small. All around the globe you'll find people have a team which they follow.

When I say most people, I really do mean lots and lots and lots of people. I know that not many follow our sort of football in the USA, poor things. But the USA is about the only major country which is not madly, daftly, in love with football.

Football is the sport followed by most people in the world, either by going to games, reading about it in newspapers or watching it on television. That's a fact.

Most people who love football follow a team. That's not quite as obvious as it might sound. There are a few who are interested in football but who don't have a particular team. They just like to see football being played. And there are others who only take an interest when there's a big game, a big competition, a big drama about to unfold.

Most of us, though, have our own team. Sometimes more than one. They will drive you potty, cause you endless grief, make you wish you had never been stuck with them.

The point of loving a team is that from time to time you will also hate this team. That's how it works. Football is the perfect example of a love-hate relationship.

So, if we agree that most people have a favourite football team, where does that team come from? I mean how do we fall in love with the team or teams we follow? Ah, that is interesting. There is no one answer to that. In fact I can think of ten.

1. *We can inherit a team*. We are born with it because our father, our mother, our nan, followed a particular team. So we do the same. It is in the blood.

2. *Where we live*. Sometimes getting your team has nothing to do with the family you are born into. It is all about where you grew up.

It could happen that no one in your family has ever followed a special team, and such families do exist, so I am told. In that case the chances are you will follow your local team, the club that plays nearest to the place or area you were born in or where you were brought up.

It's usually the same team you would have followed anyway, if you had inherited a team. But not always. For instance, as all non-Manchester United fans know, there are lots of Red Devil fans in Kent. I wonder why. Family reasons? It can't be geography. Or is it something to do with my point 3 below?

The same thing happens in Italy. Italian fans follow Juventus without ever having been to

Turin in their lives. And in Spain. You will find Real Madrid fans all over Spain.

3. *Fashion.* There are certain people who, at an age when they are easily influenced, will choose to follow a team because that team is very fashionable. And this isn't always at a young age. Adults fall for fashion as well. It usually also means that the team is successful.

So they will decide to follow this team and identify with it, because lots of other people are doing the same. It gives them status in the playground, the office, the factory, the pub. Or so they like to think.

There is nothing wrong with that, just as long as they stick with this team, even when, as will surely happen, that team becomes not quite as successful or as trendy as it used to be.

You can often tell the age of a person by the team they follow, if by chance they have acquired that team for fashionable reasons.

For example, lots of people growing up in the 1980s, in Britain and in Europe, decided to follow Liverpool – because they were a brilliant, exciting team. In the 1990s, Manchester United attracted a lot of fans from all over the country, and the globe, because they were playing so

4

well. And in the same way, for the next ten years, expect Chelsea to pick up lots of new followers, a lot of them kids wanting to be into the very latest thing that everyone is talking about. It's fashion, innit.

4. *Odd reasons*. There are also people who will deliberately choose a team which is not fashionable. This can happen at a point in their lives when they might not have a team of their own or just fancy supporting a second team. They pick upon one doing badly, whom no one in the playground or the pub seems to support.

They will decide, say, that poor old Rochdale is a joke team, with terribly small crowds. Who in their right mind will support them? So they decide they will. No, they won't actually go to their games, but they will follow their results, look out for player transfers and news. They might even go as far as to buy one of Rochdale's classic shirts. In fact, the old-style Rochdale jersey is rather pretty and unusual. The new fan might want to wear it to the pub – preferably when drunk.

When they see on television that Rochdale has managed an exciting scoreless draw at home against Grimsby, preferably while they are still standing in the pub, they will jump up and punch the air, scream out loud YES!!!! It's called following the underdog.

5. *Vague connections*. It might be that your Aunty Maisy lives in Boston in Lincolnshire. You once had a jolly nice holiday there when you were a lad. You've always had a soft spot for Boston United. Bless them.

Or let's say your first job in life took you to Perth in Scotland. You didn't know until then where Perth was. Or that it had a football team. You certainly didn't know that it was called St Johnstone. But you decided to go along one day, trying to get into the local culture. And when there you thought, 'Aye, not a bad wee team, not a bad wee ground, and an awfully nice wee town. I'll keep an eye on them from now on. Come on you Saints.'

6. *One of their players attracted you*. Rather surprisingly, this is not all that common. It should be, really, but following a team seems to come before following any of its individual players.

But it does happen. Back in the 1930s, many people became interested in, and then followed, Stoke City – purely because their star player was Stanley Matthews. In the 1950s, there were many fans of Billy Wright who started following Wolverhampton Wanderers, just because of Billy.

I know someone who follows Arsenal – though in fact he has only ever seen them once (when I gave him a spare ticket). He's a minicab driver and can't normally afford the time off, or get his hands on a ticket. He came from Ghana to London fourteen years ago and the first player he really noticed was Paul Davis, of Arsenal. So Arsenal became his team. He has an Arsenal sticker on his minicab and an Arsenal calendar in his kitchen.

I also have a friend who follows Southampton – purely because he liked the look of James Beattie. He probably fancied him, deep down, but we won't go into that. Now, Beattie has long left Southampton, but my friend remains a Southampton fan. He got sort of stuck supporting them. The tide moved on, but he decided to stay behind and be loyal to the Saints. No, not those Saints from bonny Perth this time. Different Saints. Football can be very confusing.

7. *You liked the manager*. Again, this is rare,

but I was always interested by Brian Clough and followed Nottingham Forest, just because of him. Bill Shankly also had his personal fans. José Mourinho of Chelsea will have people following his progress, transfixed by his personality, wherever he goes to in the future. Or maybe it is just the overcoat he wears that they like. Who knows?

8. *You picked a team because someone you knew liked them.* Tony Blair, our blessed Prime Minister, follows Newcastle United. That's what he has told the world. I don't think, deep down, he is a mad football fan, just a smooth politician. Although he was born in Edinburgh, he looks upon Durham as his home town. That's where he spent his early childhood and he went to school at Durham Choristers. Living in Durham, in his younger years, meant that Newcastle United became his local big team. So that's all right then. It's in line with reason 2, above, because of geography.

But what about his two older sons? Guess which team they support.

One of them follows Liverpool. Why? If you think carefully for a few moments, run through the various reasons I have already suggested, then it might strike you. No, it wasn't an Aunt Maisy who lived in Liverpool, but Tony Blair's wife, Cherie. She comes from Liverpool. So that's the reason. Euan follows Liverpool because that's where his mum comes from.

But Nicholas, the next son, is a follower of Manchester United – for reasons you would never guess.

When he was little, the Blairs had a nanny who was a mad keen Manchester United fan. She followed them, even wore their strip, and so Nicholas did too. And it has stuck.

9. *Football shirts*. Why can't that be a reason for adopting a team, if their strip is pretty, with a nice design? It's as good a reason as any.

I've always had a soft spot for Blackburn Rovers, purely because of their blue and white chequered shirts. They have changed the pattern over the decades, and today the shirts are not quite as attractive as they once were. All the same, there's still a hint of that traditional style which I do like.

I always loved the lettering on the Real Madrid shirts. I liked the style in which they wrote the names and numbers on the back of their shirts. For many years, they were done in a style like the lettering you often see stamped on wooden boxes of oranges. Now, alas, Real Madrid have changed the style. It's now an ordinary, boring sort of typeface which every club uses. I find myself not being as interested in Real Madrid as I once was.

10. *Their name*. Wolverhampton Wanderers. Don't those two long words look and sound really good?

Wolverhampton Wanderers sounds like a real name for a real football team. I'd be attracted to them, seriously, if I didn't have enough football teams that I count as my own.

Accrington Stanley, that's another brilliant name. Oh I do hope they start doing well again.

Boca Juniors is one of Argentina's most famous clubs. I've never seen them play, have never been to Argentina, but if I ever did, I'd make a point of going to a game.

I also like the sound of Newell's Old Boys. Hmm, that could be awkward. Which would I choose to watch, should I find myself in Argentina? I guess it would depend who was at home that day.

Perhaps the best sounding football names, to my ears, are Scottish ones. I love the ring of

Hamilton Academicals. Heart of Midlothian – now isn't that romantic? Queen of the South – that's another lovely name.

I do follow Queen of the South, as it happens, for reasons I will now reveal.

CHAPTER TWO

My Teams

THE FIRST REAL game I ever went to was at Ibrox in Glasgow to watch Rangers. When I was about eight or nine, I was taken by an uncle. He had no interest in football, but he took me as a birthday treat. That was good of him.

I was born in Renfrewshire, not far from Glasgow, and both my parents were Scottish. My father came from Cambuslang and my mother from Motherwell. I did once go and watch Motherwell play, at Fir Park. I went with some other boys, pushing our way to the front, crawling between legs, or being lifted over heads by friendly men.

Then for a while we lived in Dumfries. This was during the war and my father was working at an RAF maintenance station. The local team was Queen of the South. My hero became Billy Houliston, a bullet-headed centre forward who played for Queen of the South – and Scotland. He is long forgotten now, even by Scottish people. It was very rare for a Queen of the South player to be a current Scottish international. I don't think it's happened since.

By the time I was eleven, we had moved to Carlisle, which I look upon as my home town. That's where I really grew up, and where I still have relations. It's just over the border in England, but I remained passionate about Scottish football. Oh, the agonies I went through as a little boy, listening intently to the radio to hear the annual Scotland–England game. I desperately wanted Scotland to win, not only because I supported them, but also because I could boast next day in the school playground.

I cut out all the Scottish star players from the Scottish *Daily Express* – which we got each day, even though we were now living in England – and stuck them in a home-made album. For glue, I used paste made out of flour and water. The pages would be horrible and soggy at first, but then when they dried out, a strange thing happened. They hardened, rose up, as if the players were coming to life. My heroes were now standing, big and tall on the page.

I have followed the Scottish national team ever since. Don't talk about it, please. How far we have slumped in world terms. It's too sad, when I think back to the old times, the golden years. I always hope they will beat whoever they are playing, even giants like the Faroe Isles.

I still also keep an eye out, and have a soft spot for, the fortunes of Rangers, Motherwell and Queen of the South.

But once in Carlisle, I naturally began to take an interest in Carlisle United. I didn't actually go to games regularly as a boy. I couldn't afford it and my father was an invalid. Being Scottish my family was not interested in Carlisle United anyway. But when Carlisle became my adopted home town, United became my adopted team.

I did go to one of Carlisle's biggest games in my childhood. This was in 1951 when Carlisle played Arsenal at home. It was the third round of the FA Cup. Carlisle had managed a goalless draw at Highbury, so the replay was at Brunton Park. All the local schools in the area were given the half-day off because a massive crowd of 20,000 was expected. We got beaten 2–0.

Despite having terrible asthma throughout my childhood, and being small and weedy, I spent almost every spare minute playing football. I got it into my head that I wanted to be a professional footballer, if I ever grew up, which seemed unlikely.

I practised for hours in the back garden or against a wall, teaching myself to return a ball with either foot. If I was going to be a pro, as I told myself, I needed to be two-footed.

We mostly played in the streets on our council estate, under the street lights when it got dark. They were often massive games, with twenty a side. There were hardly any cars in the 1950s, not on our estate. You very rarely had to stop the game to let any traffic through. And then it was usually the coal cart or the milk float, both pulled by horses.

My first job in life was in Manchester, as a graduate trainee reporter on the old *Evening Chronicle*. One day, when Manchester United were playing Manchester City, I was told by the news editor that I was being sent to Old Trafford to cover the game.

I was terribly excited. It turned out I was to cover it from *outside* the ground, write a piece on the crowds and the atmosphere. I never did get inside to see the game.

Being a proper football reporter was a dream job. Just imagine writing about City or United, reporting their games from the lofty position of the press box, getting a free programme and free Bovril at half time. It was a job almost every Manchester journalist envied. At least I did.

I only worked in Manchester for nine months, before I came to London. I never did get into Old Trafford or City's ground of Maine Road. So I picked up no loyalty to either team. I think it might also have been due to not getting inside for that derby game. I held it against both clubs, although it wasn't their fault of course.

16

When I came to London in 1960, I was still following Carlisle United and I was still keeping an eye on my Scottish teams. But all these teams were a long way away.

So I decided I needed to have a London team, one I could go and watch, become involved with, follow their progress.

We lived in north London, and still do, in the same house we bought in 1963, so I had a choice of the two local big clubs, Spurs and Arsenal.

Arsenal was the slightly nearer. Spurs was the better team, more glamorous and exciting to watch. Best of all, they were actually winning things, like the League and Cup double in 1961.

I started going, all on my own. I have no memory of any neighbours in our street being football fans at that time. Since then, they have been creeping out of the woodwork, some for Spurs, but most of them proclaiming they have been life-long Arsenal fans.

In many ways, my decision was quite cold-blooded. I was following fashion. But once I started going, I became hooked. Spurs has been my team, my passion, for over forty years now. Alas. I took my son along, when he was old enough, and have turned him into a Spurs fan as well.

I said 'alas' because one of the probems of having 'your team', the one you become emotionally involved with, is that you go through as much pain as pleasure.

When they are ahead, you are a bag of nerves, worrying they will do something stupid. When they are behind, you are so upset, furious even, and fear a terrible defeat.

I know some Spurs fans, who have followed them for as long as me, who always leave ten minutes before the end. It's not just to avoid the traffic, but to avoid the final result. They fear it will be too difficult to cope with, win or lose. Daft, I know.

While living in London, I still followed Carlisle United. I watched them when they were playing in the London area, or at Brunton Park when I was at home in Carlisle, visiting my mother.

And then in the 1970s, a miraculous thing happened. It really was a miracle, in football terms.

Since their entry into League football in 1921, Carlisle United had always been one of nature's

Third Division North clubs. They might now and again have a modest FA Cup run, or even sneak up into the Second Division, only to fall back again. Third Division North was where they belonged.

How could they be anything other? Carlisle is a small town of only 70,000 in a remote rural region, far away from the supposed big-city heart of our national game.

In 1974, having risen through the leagues, this time without falling back, they got into the First Division. This was the top division in England, what is now the Premier League.

Even more amazing, on 24 August 1974, Carlisle United were top of the top league. I still have that league table pinned up above my desk as I write.

Only three games had been played so far that season, but even so, Carlisle had won them all – against Chelsea, Middlesbrough and Spurs.

It's an important league table I think. It means something more than just Carlisle were top. It gives hope to all teams, all players, and all of us. It proves that a small club, with small means, can rise to the top. Could it ever happen again? Hard to imagine it, when we have multi-

19

billionaires coming into the game, throwing their vast sums of money around. When the average Premiership player is earning one million pounds a year, how can a small team compete, when it can only pay its players £30,000 a year?

Carlisle's fall was just as quick as their rise. They were relegated that very same season. They then began tumbling down the leagues until in 2004, oh this is hard to write, they even fell out of the Football League altogether, dropping down into non-league.

At least in the Conference league, they had a bit of status for a change. They were seen as the Manchester United of the Conference. This was because they were getting such big crowds, around 5,000. They had a large number of travelling supporters and so put the gates up when they played away.

Carlisle, the city, was in mourning when they were demoted. As if foot and mouth, and then dramatic floods, were not bad enough disasters. A town does gain self-pride, when its local team does well. But the good news is that in 2005 they came back up again. Now they are in League Two – and doing great.

So, those are still the two teams closest to my heart – Carlisle United and Spurs. I identify with their triumphs and agonies. I suffer with them every season, and occasionally rejoice. I look upon both teams as 'our lads'.

But, I have a confession to make. When I am in London, I also go to Arsenal. Wash your mouth out, I hear true Spurs supporters cry.

I went to Highbury for years on an irregular basis, even though I had a Spurs season ticket. They never play at home on the same day, a tradition going back for decades. It helps the police in north London and, in theory, eases traffic congestion.

So when Spurs were playing away on a Saturday afternoon, too far for me to travel, I'd pop along to the Arsenal. I'd ring up a week or so before and buy a ticket, or just arrive and join the queue, both of which you could do, before the Premiership and the arrival of all-seater stadiums. Sometimes I just arrived at the last minute and bought a ticket from a tout.

Then I got hold of half a season ticket for Arsenal. This came from a friend whose son had gone to college. He didn't want to give up one of his season tickets, as there's a twenty-year wait. So I took it on, for half of each season.

My son Jake is appalled. He thinks it's disgusting to even go and watch Arsenal. How can I call myself a Spurs supporter? Even worse, in his view, is that I pay some of my money to Arsenal. I tell him I don't actually give my £600 a year to Arsenal, as such. I pay my friend. But, of course, it comes to the same thing.

My defence is that I love football first. I watch every live match on TV, which these days can mean every night of the week and twice on Saturdays and Sundays.

When I go Arsenal, I go to see a good game, good players, lots of excitement and goals – and in recent years I have not too often been disappointed, except in Europe.

I don't get upset if they lose. It does not affect me, emotionally. I like them to win, enjoy them winning, for the sake of my friends and the crowd. Unless, of course, they are playing Spurs. In that case, I will always want Spurs to win.

I also follow the England team, unless of course they are playing Scotland, which rarely happens now. Then I'll always want Scotland to beat them.

But if England are playing anyone else, I am

desperate for them to do well, which has not happened much in recent years.

As I write, I am looking forward to the 2006 World Cup. I've told my wife, as I do with every big competition, that, if there's anything she wants to say to me, say it now, pet. I won't be talking about or listening to anything except football for the next four weeks.

The year 2006 is exactly forty years since 1966. And we know what happened then. Even non-football fans, football haters even, know what happened during that glorious summer of 1966. And I was there . . .

CHAPTER THREE

Wembley, 1966

ONE OF MY PROUDEST boasts in my life is that I was there, in person, in the flesh, to witness two of the greatest events of the 1960s. One was in 1966, the other in 1967. For the second one I was on my own, a privileged on-looker when the Beatles were creating their *Sergeant Pepper* album at the Abbey Road studios.

The first was a public event, watched in person by 100,000 and by millions round the world on television. It was the summer of '66, when England beat Germany at Wembley to win the World Cup. It was the first time England had ever won it.

England might manage to do it again – I certainly hope so – but that day in 1966 can never be repeated, because Wembley, the old Wembley Stadium, known and loved by the football world, is now no more. It was knocked down in 2004 – to be rebuilt, from scratch, a new image, a new symbol, though I can't believe it will ever be as instantly recognisable as the old one.

I had been to Wembley, now and again, before 1966, and I knew about its history. Watching the FA Cup final at Wembley on TV was a national event. Even non-football fans took part, if just to mock what the footballers' wives were wearing, to see how short their miniskirts were, or how high their bee hive hair-dos.

I wasn't there for the first Wembley game on 28 April 1923. I'm not that old, but I feel I was there. I've read so much about it, seen the old photographs and newsreels, studied the old match reports.

What is rarely remembered today is that the vast structure that was Wembley Stadium was originally only one of dozens of hulking buildings on the same site. There were pavilions and exhibition halls, many of them just as splendid as the stadium. Some were devoted to a single subject, like industry. Others displayed the produce and treasures of a country, such as Australia.

There were also amusement parks, theatres, cinemas, ornamental lakes, all part of the British Empire Exhibition of 1924–25. It was created after a terrible war, to give people a chance to celebrate.

Afterwards, when the exhibition closed in 1925, almost everything was knocked down or sold off – except for the stadium itself. That stood alone, in triumphant isolation, for the next eighty years.

I have in front of me a reproduction copy of the programme for the first Wembley Cup final. I was offered an original for £90 some twenty years ago and thought 'no chance' , no one will ever pay that price. Last year, at an auction, I bid £1,000 for one in poor condition – and didn't get it.

Inside that 1923 programme, the words are just as full of hype, not to say over-the-top, as the new building it was launching.

'This vast stadium, the largest in the world, the most comfortable, the best equipped, holds more than 125,000. In area it equals the Biblical city of Jericho . . .' How did they know that?

'The British Empire Exhibition will be opened by his Majesty the King in April 1924. Come to Wembley. The British Empire Exhibition is indeed the most wonderful, the most romantic enterprise in history.'

They didn't hold back, did they, with the old bullshit – sorry, stirring words – back in 1923.

Around 200,000 turned up for the opening game between Bolton Wanderers and West Ham – and most managed to squeeze in. Many got in illegally, spilling on to the pitch. Disaster was averted by the calm work of a policeman, PC George Scorey, on a white horse called Billy. He herded the crowd and moved them back safely so the match could begin. To this day, the first Wembley game – won by Bolton two-nil – is often still referred to as the 'White Horse Final'.

From the beginning, it was planned that

Wembley Stadium would hold a variety of events, not just football. One of the first non-sporting events was a rodeo held in 1924, part of the Empire Exhibition excitements.

In 1948, the Olympics took place at Wembley, and now they are coming back to London in 2012. The new Wembley Stadium will, I am sure, play its own part in the story of those games.

Wembley has hosted many big speedway events and major boxing matches, such as Cassius Clay's clash with Henry Cooper in 1963. In 1975, Evel Knievel demonstrated how to jump thirteen double decker buses on a motor bike, but not very well. He crashed on landing and injured his spine.

Perhaps the most famous non-sporting event took place on 13 July 1985 and was watched by millions round the world. Live Aid was the event which helped to get Bob Geldof his honorary knighthood and started a trend for pop stars to show us their finer feelings by helping less fortunate mortals.

But mostly, when we think of Wembley, we think of football – and we think of 1966.

I always loved arriving at Wembley, spotting the Twin Towers in the distance from the tube train. Then walking down Wembley Way with the hordes, all good natured, enjoying themselves, having a treat, a day out. I never saw violence or nastiness at the old Wembley. The stadium itself always seemed to unite rival fans, teams and nations in the same spirit.

Then you went up some rather horrid open concrete staircases, round some dingy grey concrete corridors, climbed some nasty steps, till suddenly there was the pitch, and the roar.

I have to admit that Wembley, over the years, had been allowed to decay and crumble. The seats, the facilities, the structure generally had become old, crummy and unpleasant. It was long overdue for some improvement. But in 1966, I don't remember anything unpleasant or crummy. It was all wonderful.

This was partly due to the fact that I had an excellent ticket that day. I was in K section, Entrance 36, Row 9, Seat 37, price £5, one of the best seats in the house. In the new Wembley, a top seat will cost you about £1,000. For that money in 1966, you could have bought two Minis or a small terrace house.

I got it through a friend who was a television executive, James Bredin, boss of Border TV in Carlisle. He even arranged for me to go there in his chauffeur-driven car. So on that occasion, I didn't go on the tube as I normally did. But I still looked out for the Twin Towers from afar, and my heart gave a little flutter.

The awful thing is – I can't remember a great deal about the game itself. It all went in a flash, as of course it did for the players.

But recently, I watched a BBC video of the game.

The first surprise was the quality of the film. It is in black and white, with no action replays or incredible close-ups, but you can see everything clearly. And the accent of the commentator, Kenneth Wolstenholme, was not all that dated, no more than Peter Drury's is on ITV. No advertising hoardings could be seen except for *Radio Times* on the scoreboard – no sponsors' logos on the players' shirts. What an innocent, uncommercial age it was. Every player had the same hair, short back and sides, except for Bobby Charlton's sweep-over. All shorts were incredibly short, almost up to their bollocks. The crowd wore rosettes and did a lot

30

of clapping, but very limited singing, apart from 'Oh when the reds go marching in'. And there was only limited chanting, 'Ingland' or 'Attack, Attack'. No swear words. When the crowd didn't like the ref, they sang, 'Oh, oh, what a referee'. Today it's very different. 'Who's that wanker in the black?' is one of the milder comments you might hear.

In 1966, when the Germans chanted 'Deutschland', we replied with 'England'. Today, it's more likely to be 'You're gonna win fuck all'.

It rained in the second half, yet in my mind the sun shone all day long and the Wembley pitch was perfect, as always. The England team are now all giants, but on the day they were so thin and wiry. Nobby Stiles looked like he hadn't eaten anything in weeks. It must have been the war rations, observed my wife. He made Lee Bowyer look like Mr Universe. There was nobody in the England team who you would call big and strong, unlike John Terry or Sol Campbell today. Jack Charlton was tall, but giraffe-like, awkward rather than hefty. You don't get such clumsy, awkward England players today, not since Carlton Palmer.

31

They all looked incredibly fit, despite players' diets being rubbish in those days. We are told they used to eat half a cow before kick-off. They did tire, though, and well before the end. With no subs, they were all knackered in extra time, except for Alan Ball. He was amazing, running non-stop.

There were no nasty tackles, no diving, no pretending, no pushing and shoving, no arguing with the ref. Players helped each other up and shook hands. It was, after all, a World Cup final. Players realised they were on show.

As for the skills, the passing, the control, the movements, I would say the quality of the England team today is not appreciably better than forty years ago. The Dutch master, Johan Cruyff, had not yet invented his swivel turn (that wasn't until the 1970s), but almost all the other fancy bits were there. For instance, bringing the ball down on your instep, overlapping full-backs, clever back heels. Our full-backs were poor, as they are today, with Ray Wilson giving away the first goal, but the rest of the team were excellent, not a weak link.

I interviewed Bobby Charlton a couple of years ago, and his memory was of hardly being in the match. He and Beckenbauer had been detailed to mark each other, so cancelled one another out, but Bobby had a very good game. His passing was as good as Beckham's, but he could also shoot from any distance. Bobby Moore was elegant, but I'd forgotten his chest control, how it gave him so much space to come forward.

Germany had lots of possession, some good movement, but England took their chances and deserved to win. For the first time, I properly understood Wolstenholme's now famous words: 'They think it's all over – it is now!' I was there, so didn't hear him say them. I'd assumed it referred to the ref blowing the final whistle, but he says the second part as Hurst scores – to make it 4–2 meaning England had now definitely won.

I loved watching it. My memory had not played tricks. The England team in 1966 were excellent.

CHAPTER FOUR

George Best

To Hunter
Best Wishes
George Best

MANCHESTER UNITED 1967-68

FUNNY HOW OFTEN FOOTBALLERS have apt surnames, which sum them up or describe them in some way. Frank Swift, from my childhood, was a very quick goalkeeper. Today, both Robbie Keane and Roy Keane are very enthusiastic players. While Robbie Savage is well, er, I'll leave that to you.

George Best is probably the top of the lot for having the most appropriate name. Thinking back over all the British players I have watched, in the flesh, on the pitch, I can't think of anyone I enjoyed watching more.

There are three or four foreign players in the last few decades who were probably better – Pele, Cruyff, Maradona for instance. Most fans around the world would pick them ahead of Best in the World's Best Eleven to play Mars. But I deliberately said *British*. I'm also thinking of players I personally saw playing on a regular basis. I never saw Pele play, in the flesh, just on TV. I only saw Cruyff and Maradona in internationals.

I did meet Cruyff once when he was manager at Barcelona. I went to the post-match press conference at the Nou Camp. It was held in a large lecture hall. All the reporters sat at desks as if they were at school. Cruyff spoke to them from a raised platform. What was amazing was that he was fielding questions in Spanish, Dutch and English, and answering each one in the appropriate language. George Best, for all his native wit, could never manage that.

George never played or lived abroad, though he might well have done, if he had played a couple of decades later. And he never played in any World Cup or European Nations Cup – for the simple reason that he played for Northern Ireland – though he might have done, if the timing had been different. Northern Ireland did make the World Cup finals in 1958 and 1982. It was George's bad luck, and Northern Ireland's, that his years at the top were in the middle of a very bad period for his country.

George was born in Belfast on 22 May 1946. I first interviewed him in 1965 when he was just nineteen and had got into the Manchester United first team. He was being hailed as the new boy wonder.

In football, since it all began, we have had boy wonders, every year or so. There is nothing unique about that. George was attracting wonder and attention on the football field because of his incredible, natural ball skills, gliding down the wing and leaving hardened defenders on their backs. Unlike Cristiano Ronaldo today, on the wing for Manchester United, Best didn't get carried away by his own tricks, doing too many step-overs and losing the ball. Best was much more direct, either going for goal, laying on a cross or a pass, or scoring himself.

George Best was also attracting attention off the pitch. This was the mid 1960s, the era of Beatlemania. George had a Beatle haircut and dark good looks. Lots of girls were already fancying him. At the age of just nineteen, however, and as a newcomer in the first team, he was being a good boy, disciplined, obedient.

I interviewed him in his digs, after training. What he told me then sounds so innocent and naive today. But that's what he was, more or less, at that time anyway. Here's what he said.

'When I first went to the ground and I'd seen all those big lads, I thought, there's no chance here. I'll never make the grade. I was fifteen and sharing digs with another Belfast boy. After two weeks, I packed up and went home. I was just so homesick.

'But my father talked me into coming back, and I stayed. I've changed a lot since those days. If somebody in a shop gave me change out of ten bob and I'd given them a pound, I'd be too shy to complain.

'You've got to have confidence to be a footballer. I think in the last two months I've got it. I used to lie in my bed on Friday nights, imagining how I was going to beat everybody.

Funny, I never did badly, always well, when I was doing this thinking. Now I never think about the match at all.

'I used to wear very quiet clothes. Now, if I see something smart, no matter what anybody else says, I buy it. I've got a black and white striped jacket. The lads in the team are always saying, "Here comes the butcher."

'I used to write home three or four times a week. Now, well, I haven't written at all for a few weeks. It's terrible. That's one thing I've gone down on.

'But I can talk to my parents, the way I never used to, as if I'm grown up. I can talk about girls. I never had the nerve before.

'I thought I wouldn't be able to talk to Denis Law and Bobby Charlton, the ones I'd always hero-worshipped as a kid. But your opinion changes. They're just like ordinary blokes in the street.

'They're all married in the first team, so after training I get a bit bored. I thought at first they didn't want me to mix. They do, but they've got families. The afternoons, I either play snooker or go bowling and I go to the pictures perhaps twice a week. I'm getting very lazy. I read a bit:

horror stories, comics, that sort of thing.

'I don't drink or smoke. Perhaps on a rare occasion, I might have a lager. Then it gets back to the boss, Mr Busby, that you're drunk. I share digs with another footballer. I would like to have a flat on my own. But the boss thinks there might be temptation. Perhaps, when I'm twenty-one. I've no complaints. I like my landlady.

'One thing you never realise until you actually play is that other footballers are always talking to you on the pitch, though no one else can hear. One bloke, every time he got near me, said, "Get your hair cut, scruff." They try to nark you, break you down.

'I've found that footballers never read reports of their own matches. They're just not interested. They *know* what happened. I read them. I'm young.

'I save most of my money. Last week's £175 was very unusual – I had three matches, one an international. Often it's down to £50 a week.

'What I'd like to be is a millionaire, that's what I'd like. If it meant not playing football again from this minute on? Well, perhaps I don't want to be a millionaire after all.'

*

In 1968, Manchester won the European Champions Cup, the first English club to do so (though Celtic had won it in 1967). Best's display that day earned him the title in the Portuguese press of 'El Beatle'. He won the League championship twice with Manchester United. In 1968, he was also elected European Footballer of the Year.

George became football's first modern super-star, in the sense that he became a household name, even in households that had no interest in football. He was hired to do modelling, had a chain of boutiques named after him, became a style icon, a sex symbol. He was followed everywhere by the paparazzi. His latest clothes, his hair, his girlfriends, real or alleged, were endlessly chronicled. This was all long before the world had heard of David Beckham.

But by 1972, aged only twenty-six, when footballers in theory are approaching their peak, his career was already on a downward slope. This was mainly due to temptations and distractions off the pitch, of the type Mr Busby must have talked to him about when George mentioned wanting to get a flat on his own –

drink, money, women. All the usual things that can distract young lads, if they are so lucky.

George started turning up late for training at Manchester United. That is, if he turned up at all. He would go on benders that would last for days. The coaches would send out search parties, unable to find him.

I was sent up to Manchester once, around this time, with a TV crew in order to interview him. He had agreed to a time and place, but when we got there, there was no sign of him. We went round Manchester looking for him, in night-clubs or houses where he might be asleep, but no luck.

The producer of the programme was John Birt – later a big cheese at the BBC, and now Lord Birt. I rang him in London to say that's it, I'm fed up, I'm not being messed around any more by some idiot, drunken footballer, I'm coming home. John persuaded me, and the crew, to stay on another night. Next day we did track George down and got our interview.

Although I was pissed off by being messed around, at the same time I rather admired George for his devilish attitude – to the media as well as his coaches.

All the old football reporters, once his behaviour became well known, were going tut tut, how disgusting, what a terrible example for younger players. They were writing editorials and columns on the sports pages, all a bit pompous and self-righteous. I was amused by his antics. Many coaches, then and now, are rather brutal, nasty people. They scream and shout abuse at their young charges, trying to turn them into robots who will do what they are told.

George, meanwhile, continued to be unreliable at training but then on the match day, still hungover, he would stagger on to the pitch and play a blinder. Well, a lot of the time.

It obviously couldn't go on and in 1973, Manchester United let him go, realising there was little chance of reforming him.

He then had various loan or short-term spells, at Fulham, in Scotland, in Ireland. He also turned up in the North American league. He was asked why he had gone to North America and replied, 'Because I saw a sign saying "Drink Canada Dry".'

The most famous story told about George may or may not be true, but because of how he acted, it is totally believable. It could be true.

George has gone on a bender and wakes up in a posh London hotel next to a naked and gorgeous Miss World. Around the room are several empty bottles of champagne. On the bedside table is a large wad of cash someone has given him.

A waiter knocks and enters the bedroom, bringing more champagne. He sees George, Miss World, the empty bottles, the money.

'George,' says the waiter, 'where did it all go wrong . . .?'

George did wreck his own career, abuse his talents, leaving the game long before he should have done. He would have played much longer, if he had been a sensible, sober clean-living player like Bobby Charlton or Gary Lineker. But he had fun and brought a lot of pleasure to a lot of fans.

A couple of years ago, I spent some time with him again, this time in an Italian restaurant in Chelsea. He looked fit and well, despite all his current health problems. That day he was holding a bleeper, ready for a call from a hospital for a liver transplant. They had to wait for a sudden death, probably in a road accident, and the availability of a suitable healthy liver to replace George's worn out, bashed up liver. (He did get a new one, successfully, then went on the drink again, having said he never would. He fell ill again in October 2005 and died the following month. A sad loss to football and the country.)

When I met him that day, before he had the transplant, he didn't look bad for his age. No more worn or grey and lined than most men in their sixties.

I chatted with him about his 1960s days, how I had first met him when he was aged only nineteen. He said at that time, at his height in the 1960s, he didn't actually make a lot of money, despite all the advertising and promotions. The money in football wasn't all that amazing, not like today. He estimated that in 1968, his best year, he made no more than £30,000. Half of that was from football, the other half from off-the-field sources.

Today, of course, a star like Best would have done as well if not better than Beckham and be making £10 million a year. If, of course, he had stayed sober and sensible and actually turned up to fashion and promotional shoots, as well as training.

But a strange thing has happened in football these last few years. Icons from the past, if they are still with us and able to manage a few words, and sign their name, can make a huge amount of money.

Books by and about George Best appear to have been coming out every year for the last forty years. The demand for George was still there right up to his death. Newspapers wanted him for quotes and he acted as a football pundit on TV. He even got asked to put his name to football boots, when he hadn't pulled one on for decades.

I don't know how much he earned over recent years, but I guess it was about ten times more than it was in the 60s. George Best was one of football's legends.

CHAPTER FIVE

The History of Football

ENGLAND, OR MORE ACCURATELY Britain, gave football to the world in 1863. Hurrah, hurrah. We might not be world beaters any more but we beat the world in getting football organised, with proper rules and regulations. We created the game which the whole world plays today.

Kicking and throwing some sort of ball or round object is a natural thing to do. I'm sure the moment we walked out of the caves, on our own, on two legs, there were blokes kicking or chucking things around. They could have used round stones, hard nuts, handy bits of wood. Even balls of rubber taken from trees. They either chucked them at each other or competed to see who could kick or throw the object furthest or most accurately.

There are stories and drawings that offer proof of some sort of ball games taking place in ancient China, ancient Greece and ancient Mexico. But we don't know what the rules were.

In medieval Europe, there were few rules. Just two teams, of sometimes 100 people, who would charge up and down a village street after a ball. The object was to get it from one end of the street, or the village, to another. Along the way, they beat up anyone they could in the rival gang.

So if humans had been playing some sort of football, all over the globe, for ever and ever, how come it was in England in 1863 that it got itself organised?

Two reasons, really. One was our public schools, the big famous ones we know today, such as Eton, Harrow, Charterhouse, Rugby. They were actually at a pretty low point in the mid-nineteenth century. The number of pupils was small and the system offered limited education in sometimes brutal conditions. Then a series of hearty headmasters began to take over, most of them church people, who saw their schools' ancient football games as a healthy activity for young boys. It might distract them from anti-social, or perhaps even more disgusting, personal habits.

Each school had its own code of football, often played in courtyards, with the walls as boundaries.

These muscular Christian teachers created proper rules, organised inter-house competitions, gave caps and awards to victors and champions.

When these ex-public school boys went up to Oxford and Cambridge, they wanted to carry on playing football, but found that other schools had slightly different rules.

In 1848 at Cambridge, a group of chaps from five different schools met to arrange one set of rules for football. This way, boys from the different schools could all play together.

This first set of rules has not survived. But it's clear that at this stage in football's development you could still catch the ball with your hands, though you then had to play it with your feet. You could hack down another player from behind, or anyway you liked. Football was seen as a man's game, played roughly and brutally. But goals, and the scoring of them, had been established, and by around 1860, the number of players per side had settled down to eleven.

In 1863 came the big breakthrough. Twelve different football clubs met together in a tavern in London to set down once and for all a proper set of rules. And so the Football Association was born. Most of these twelve clubs were in and around the London area, filled with ex-public school or Oxbridge chaps.

By 1866, handling the ball, except for the goalkeeper, had been banned. Violently tackling a player when he didn't happen to have the ball was outlawed. And I should think so too.

The FA began its FA Challenge Cup in 1872 and in the same year set up the world's first international match, between England and Scotland. The score was 0–0.

For most of the next few decades, Scotland

thumped England regularly – partly because Scotland had invented the idea of passing the ball. It sounds obvious. But in the English public school version, one player, said to be the best dribbler, charged up the field at the head of a pack. When he lost the ball, the other pack charged the other way. Scottish players found that passing the ball between themselves was a much easier way of getting up the park, and keeping it away from the other lot.

One of the key figures in the early days of the FA was a posh bloke called the Hon Arthur Kinnaird, later Lord Kinnaird. He was a big red-bearded Scotsman with a large estate in Perthshire. He played in nine Cup finals and was known for his forceful style of play, much to the worry of his mother.

'I'm afraid Arthur will come home one day with a broken leg,' his mother observed to a visitor from the FA, Sir Francis Marindin.

'Don't worry,' said Marindin, 'it will not be his own.'

Football did not become a national activity, or a professional sport, or even have a proper league system, until the arrival of the industrial working classes on the scene in the 1880s.

Factory teams had grown up in the North, often founded by church people or ex-public school boys. As they got better, playing further afield, some of their players were found to be receiving money in their back pocket or in their boots. According to FA rules, this was totally illegal and against all the public school, amateur, gentlemanly ways of doing things.

In 1888, a group of the leading northern clubs met together to set up the Football League. The gents from the FA had somehow never got round to organising a proper league competition, with points and league tables. They had concentrated instead on either the FA Cup or endless series of friendlies.

The league was the idea of a Scotsman, William McGregor from Aston Villa, who arranged the meeting.

The first ever football league comprised just twelve teams – Aston Villa, Accrington Stanley, Blackburn Rovers, Bolton Wanderers, Burnley, Derby County, Everton, Notts County, Preston North End, Stoke City, West Bromwich Albion and Wolverhampton Wanderers.

All were professional clubs, which had finally been given the okay by the FA in 1885. Six were

HUNTER DAVIES

from Lancashire. The rest from around the Midlands.

Notice the absence of today's three big clubs. Manchester United were not formed until 1902. Mind you, the team of railway workers they developed out of, Newton Heath, dated back to 1878. Arsenal did not become Arsenal till 1914, though they had existed since 1886 when some workers at the Royal Arsenal munitions works at Woolwich started a club. Chelsea was not formed till 1905.

The other important element, which explains why Britain gave football to the world when it did, was that we were the first industrial nation. So when football became popular with the workers, they went along in their masses on Saturday afternoons, when the factories closed. This provided more money for better facilities, proper stadiums, bigger transfer fees.

Railways were first created in Britain, as part of the industrial revolution, long before they reached Europe. Fans were able to travel miles by train and tram to get to the big games. Each year, London was swamped by northern hordes, down for the Cup final.

By 1900, football had become pretty much as

52

we know it today. It was played then in mostly the same stadiums as it is today. Corner kicks had been introduced in 1873, crossbars instead of bits of tape appeared in 1875. Referees, complete with whistle, arrived in 1878. Penalty kicks and nets came in 1891. By now, teams were arranged into defenders, half backs and forwards.

Players wore baggy shorts, thick jumpers, heavy boots, and the ball was made of leather. In wet or muddy conditions, the ball got heavier as the game wore on.

But essentially, football was the game we know now. A football fan, arriving today from the terraces of 1900, would have to sit, but he could easily watch and understand a modern match. Just as we could go back a hundred years and get as much pleasure as we do now. The offside rule is simpler today, in theory. But that's about the only major difference.

The players of course were poorly paid, earning a maximum weekly wage in 1901 of £4. At the time, the ordinary working man was on £2 a week. Roughly speaking, for the next sixty years, the normal professional footballer was earning only double the wage of a skilled craftsman. In 1961 the maximum wage was £20. It was then that it was decided that having a cap on the amount a player could earn was unfair. And so that rule was stopped.

Nonetheless, while players in the olden days lived much the same lives as their neighbours, in the same sort of houses, with the same sort of lifestyle, the star players did become heroes. Their faces appeared on cigarette cards and in other illustrations and when they retired, they could usually afford to buy or manage a pub or a sweet shop, using their name as an attraction.

From the beginning of professional football, people were moaning about rubbish referees and too much violence on the pitch. Just like today.

As for the money, the football world was appalled in 1905 by the first ever £1,000 transfer. This was when Alf Common was transferred from Sunderland to Middlesbrough. It was seen as the end of football, as they knew it. The game was being ruined by money.

Alf Common was a tubby, jovial player known for his practical jokes and his attempts to lose weight. Sounds very like another north-easterner, P. Gascoigne.

Britain began exporting football almost from the moment it was invented. As early as the 1870s, British citizens living abroad, visiting sailors and railway workers, were introducing football to Denmark, Holland and France. By the 1890s, Brits had even taken the game to South America.

All over the world today, you still see leading foreign teams with decidedly English names, such as Grasshoppers of Zurich or Old Boys in South America. The descriptions of the game, such as the word for goal or penalty, corner or foul, are often the very same in other languages. Although they might be said in a different way.

The idea of fair play, the word and what it means, also appears all over the world. This goes back to those early public school, amateur teams, such as the Corinthians.

The Corinthians upheld the purest values which meant they would never take part in a game for money or even for any prizes. They never argued with the referee and if the other team happened to lose a man, because of injury or being sent off, they would play with ten men – just to keep it fair. Ah, those were the days.

CHAPTER SIX

The Glory Game

a preview of

THE GLORY GAME

an anatomy of
a year with a
football club by

HUNTER DAVIES

to be published by
Weidenfeld & Nicolson
in October

PEOPLE WERE WRITING ABOUT football almost from the moment it was invented, though at first in a very gentlemanly way. Charles Alcock, the first secretary of the FA, produced the first *Football Annual* in 1868. Football annuals, in their various forms, have continued to this day, the best known being *Rothmans*, though these days it's been taken over by Sky Sports.

Newspapers were slow at first to take much

interest in football, despite the fact that in the 1880s there were three daily sporting newspapers – *Sporting Chronicle*, *Sporting Life* and the *Sportsman*. They were mainly devoted to horse racing.

Once the Football League began in 1888, and a proper professional competition was up and running, with regular games and a league table, the sporting newspapers quickly realised something new had happened. They had to cover it.

A new breed of human activity was then born – football reporters. The first recorded press box, created specially for these new animals, was built by Celtic in 1894.

For generations, right up until a decade ago, one of the highlights of the football week for many fans was the 'Pink 'Un'. This was a newspaper produced at incredible speed each Saturday afternoon, containing, if you were lucky, all that afternoon's football results. They were called Pink 'Uns even though some were green and some blue, because they were printed on coloured paper, to stand out from the ordinary week-day newspapers. Every city in Britain of any size, big enough to have its own local paper, had its own special football Pink.

The match reports were often very confused and garbled, not to say very funny. The reporter would be dictating copy on the phone, shouting it out, line by line, minute by minute, as the game was progressing, not of course knowing what the outcome was going to be. But they were printed so quickly that often you could read all the results while still on the way home from a game. Modern computer technology in many ways has slowed down rather than speeded up news in newspapers.

Today, of course, Saturday afternoon football editions of the local newspapers have all but disappeared. This is because the news comes from lots of different places now – TV and radio, mobiles and computers, live football programmes and even whole channels devoted to sport.

Now and again, in the 1960s and 1970s, I did an occasional football report for the *Sunday Times*. I worked in other departments, but being a football fan, I would often beg the sports editor to let me cover a game.

I had never realised how hard it was to do a match report. You have to produce a sensible account that people can understand. It had to have the correct goal scorers, the major incidents, written and repeated down the phone within half an hour of the game being over. In those days, fighting for a phone was about the toughest part. Then you had to tell it all to some long-suffering and very bored copytaker at the other end who would say, at every pause, 'Is that it?'

Today, it's a bit easier. All reporters have their own laptops and direct access to their sports desks and into the computer.

In 1972, I did a book called *The Glory Game*. This was about a year in the life of Tottenham Hotspur. Looking back, I don't know how I got away with it, how I got inside the club and managed to gain the sort of access no football reporter would ever get today.

I suppose they didn't really know me. That partly explains how I got started. I just hung around, until I was accepted. I wasn't a regular football reporter, someone who might have written something nasty about them in the past.

I never had a contract with the club, though I told all the players they could read what I wrote about them. And I promised to share the proceeds with the first-team pool.

I started with them right at the beginning of the new season. Actually before the season started – in pre-season training. Bill Nicholson, the manager, normally a very dour, silent Yorkshireman, let me go on runs with them, be out on the training ground with them, wear their training strip, take showers with them afterwards.

During the season itself, I sat on the bench at away games, beside Bill and the coaches. At half time, and after all the games, I followed them into the dressing room. I travelled with the team in their private compartments on the train. Clubs didn't have luxury coaches in those days. When they played abroad, I went on their private chartered plane. I visited the homes of all the players and was invited to their private parties.

All the time, I expected something to go wrong. I feared there would be a scene in the dressing room one day, some row, cups flying, and Bill would glare around, catch my face, an interloper, and chuck me out. My book might then be all over.

I used to think to myself that, if it does happen, at least I will have had the first-hand experience of being in the dressing room with top players during a top game. As an ordinary fan on the terraces, this was something I had always dreamed about.

But I did get it finished, and handed it in. Several people at the publishers didn't expect it to sell well, not outside London N17, the heartland of Spurs. They said no Arsenal fan would be interested for a start. Nor many fans of other teams. I tried to say I didn't see it as peculiar to one team, one club, or even one period. It was for all football fans – a behind-the-scenes look at any club, anywhere, at any time.

It's still in print today, after all these years – in both the UK and the USA, which is even more surprising. Most of the names of the players are not known today. They wore flared trousers, earned only £200 a week and lived in £20,000 semis on new estates.

It's hard to imagine such a book being possible today. All Premiership players now have their own agents, lawyers, accountants and their own individual promotional deals,

TV, radio and publishing arrangements. Clubs also have loads of press officers and marketing men. You just couldn't get the access. As for getting inside a dressing room, no chance.

One of the things I did in *The Glory Game* was a series of surveys of the first-team pool. It was really a way of using up all the facts and figures I hadn't quite managed to work into the book itself.

I asked them, among other things, about their educational qualifications, if any; the sort of house they lived in; what car they drove. The most popular car, driven by five of them, was a Jaguar, followed by a Mini, three, and an MGB GT, two.

I listed their business interests, outside football. Half didn't have any at all. Several had invested in a sports shop. One of them, the late Cyril Knowles, owned a fish and chip shop. I don't think any Premiership player has one of those today.

Outside football, their main interest was playing golf, which has not changed. As for their newspaper reading habits, out of eighteen, thirteen put the *Sun* as their first choice. I should think that has not changed either.

I also asked them at what point in their lives they had enjoyed their football most. Was it at fifteen, when they had just left school? Or was it now, when they were supposed to be at the very top? Over sixty per cent said they had enjoyed it much more at fifteen. Despite the fame and good wages, the pressures and strains of being in the First Division were just too much.

Today, even though modern Premiership footballers are on fabulous wages, I suspect that even more than sixty per cent would say the pleasure in actually playing football is not what it was when they were young. Sad, really.

CHAPTER SEVEN

Dwight Yorke

BRITAIN EXPORTED FOOTBALL TO the world. In the nature of things, what goes round, comes around, sometimes to haunt you.

Until the 1950s, all Britain's national teams and big clubs felt superior to any foreign team. After all, it was our game. Then came the 6–3 hammering that Hungary gave England in

1953. It made everyone realise that these foreigners might well be on to something.

Until then, we knew very little about foreign players and foreign play. One exception was the visit of Moscow Dynamo to Britain in 1945 to play some friendly games. They got a great deal of attention. Over 90,000 watched them play Glasgow Rangers at Ibrox, and 82,000 came to Stamford Bridge for their game against Chelsea.

Very few individual foreigners had ever played their football in Britain. From about the 1900s, there had only been the odd one or two. A German, somehow washed up on our shores, did play for Chelsea in 1907. An Egyptian turned out for Fulham in 1911. An Italian appeared for Reading in 1913. But these were very rare sightings.

In 1931, the FA made it almost impossible for foreigners to play for our clubs by placing restrictions on any professional player. They had to have lived in the UK for at least two years. This lasted till 1976. South Africans often found it a bit easier, their country being part of the Empire.

The best known foreign-born player in the post-war years was the magnificent Bert

Trautmann, Manchester City's well-loved goalie. He helped them win the FA Cup in 1956, despite playing with a broken neck. At the end of that season, he was voted Footballer of the Year, the first foreigner to receive that honour.

The reason that Trautmann could play was because he had been a German prisoner-of-war in England. Not a course of action which is normally recommended, but he'd been here for several years.

The modern wave of foreign players is generally agreed to have begun in 1978 when Spurs signed Ossie Ardiles and Ricardo Villa. They had been part of Argentina's World Cup-winning squad. Around 10,000 fans turned up to see them on their first day at training.

I happened by chance to report their first game, against Nottingham Forest. My match report was headlined 'Vamos Vamos Boys'. Everyone was enormously impressed by Ardiles, by his intelligence, skills, directness.

Today, of course, in the Premiership, about one third of all the players are foreign. In fact it can often happen, as with Chelsea and Arsenal, that the whole team, including the five subs, are all foreign-born players.

The other striking feature of modern British football is the proportion of black players. As with foreigners, that was something hardly ever seen in our football until the 1970s.

But like the foreign-born players, if you study the records closely enough, you'll see there always was the odd one or two.

The first black player on these shores is now believed to have been Andrew Watson. He was born in Georgetown, British Guiana (now Guyana). He played for Queen's Park, the Scottish amateur club, in 1874, and also toured with Corinthians.

The first black professional player was Arthur Wharton who joined Preston North End in 1889. He was born in Ghana, the son of a Methodist missionary.

The post-war wave of immigrants from the West Indies, invited over here to run our trains and hospitals, meant that by the 1970s there was a large supply of British-born black players, speaking native tongues, like cockney or brummy.

In 1978, Viv Anderson of Nottingham Forest became the first black player to appear for the full England team.

*

In 1998, I was approached to write the biography of Dwight Yorke of Manchester United, a player born in the West Indies.

I had always been fascinated by the culture shocks foreign players must feel when they come over here. They have to adapt to our climate, our social and cultural conditions, and all the obvious prejudices. How had Dwight coped and managed to come through to the very top of his profession?

I was particularly impressed by the fact that Dwight's agent was Tony Stephens – who was also the agent for David Beckham, Michael Owen and Alan Shearer.

Dwight was born in Tobago on 3 November 1971. Tobago is a small, remote, rural island, just 27 miles long with a population of 50,000. The West Indies has never had a tradition of playing football, even with its long connection with the British Empire. Cricket has always been its national game.

Not many West Indians, unless they were second generation, born here in Britain, have appeared in British teams. The nearest is probably John Barnes, born in Jamaica. Like

Dwight, he is fluent, intelligent, well spoken. He came to England as a little boy and went to school here, unlike Dwight.

When Dwight was aged two in Tobago, he nearly died. He was hit by a car outside his house. He was carried by the car's bonnet for about 100 yards before it ran over him. He had a broken leg, bad burns, and was in hospital for over three months. His mother, being a good Christian woman, prayed for a miracle recovery. He did survive, though he has burn marks on his back to this day.

He had eight brothers and sisters and a father who was rarely ever around. The family was very poor and Dwight could not afford football boots or a proper ball.

When I went over to Tobago, along with Dwight to visit his mother, she was still in the same house, though now expanded with fake Georgian windows and extra bedrooms.

She showed me a calabash. It is a bit like a coconut and is the fruit of the calabash tree. It is perfectly round but very hard and it is what Dwight kicked around as a little boy, instead of a ball. It must have been hellish uncomfortable for a six-year-old kid to kick around with bare feet.

By the time he was eight, Dwight's skills were already being spotted by a local man who ran a Saturday morning football school. By the age of ten, Dwight was playing for the Trinidad and Tobago under-14 national team. (Trinidad is the big sister island, but they count as one country.)

Dwight was good at all sports, and at the age of sixteen was thinking of applying to go to the USA on a sports scholarship, to a black Southern college which specialised in attracting West Indian athletes. If he had done so, he would probably have been lost to soccer for ever.

He knew nobody in the professional soccer world, nor did anyone at that time in Tobago have contacts with any British clubs. Their scouts had never got that far.

But then there came a stroke of luck. Out of the blue in 1989, Aston Villa arrived to make a brief tour of Trinidad and Tobago. It was something Villa had never done before. And it was all arranged at practically the last minute.

Villa had just come up into the First Division and were struggling to find their feet. In March 1989, an England friendly game had been arranged, for the national team. Villa realised they had ten days free, with no league games on. At short notice, they decided they would have a mid-season break, to perk up the players.

It was by chance they chose to play a couple of exhibition games against Trinidad and Tobago. That was apparently the best offer they could get, at short notice, if they wanted a break in the sun.

When Graham Taylor, Villa's manager, saw the seventeen-year-old Dwight playing against them, he said to his coach, 'By God, that kid can play.'

They arranged to give him a plane ticket to come over to Birmingham for a trial. Later that year they signed him for a fee of £10. They also donated £10,000 to Dwight's club in Tobago.

'In thirty years of football,' so Graham told me, 'I've seen a lot of lads who are good at sixteen and seventeen. Then they drop. But with Dwight, I thought he's got a chance. He's got hunger and the confidence.'

Dwight arrived in a Birmingham winter, never having seen snow before. He knew nobody and was put into digs.

After just six months at Villa, with Dwight

having worked hard and having made his first-team debut, manager Graham Taylor suddenly left. He had become the England manager. Taylor had been Dwight's mentor and discoverer.

Ron Atkinson, who later took over as Villa manager, dropped Dwight from the team. Brian Little, the next manager, saved his career. John Gregory was also a fan, but was forced in August 1998 to let him go to Manchester United for £12.6 million.

When I was writing his book, Dwight was at the very height of his powers. He became top goalscorer in the Premier League and was a vital part of the Manchester United team that won the famous treble. He played in that dramatic game against Bayern Munich in May 1999, before a crowd of 90,000 in Barcelona, to win the European Champions League.

The book therefore had a brilliant football story and also an excellent human one. Alas, I have to admit it was pretty much a failure.

I never managed to get close to Dwight himself. He was making so much money, having so much success and fame, he didn't appear much interested in his own book. He was always cancelling or turning up late for our appointments.

I went to see him once, at his vast mansion in Cheshire, where he lived totally alone. I couldn't get in. I hadn't realised I needed a security number to even speak into the intercom at his front gate. He'd forgotten to give me the code. I did have his phone number, but that day I didn't have my own mobile. I banged and banged. I could see his Ferrari and knew he must be inside. I had to walk about a mile to find a public phone. I rang him and told him to open the bloody front gate.

When he eventually did let me in, he was with an attractive young blonde woman. They said they had been in the bedroom, measuring up. She was an interior decorator, giving him advice. I believed every word.

Apart from such distractions in his life, the most important single thing about him, which I never knew when I began the book, is that he is a totally private person. He gave nothing away about his inner feelings, hopes, fears.

He was always charming, intelligent, never bad-mouthed anyone. I just failed to get close to him. I think this was the quality which had helped him survive. He had built up a protection against the outside world.

His career is nearing its end now, having moved to play for a club in Australia. As a footballer, he did brilliantly, playing at the top in the Premiership for over eighteen years, including later spells at Blackburn Rovers and Birmingham City.

Now, as I write, he has perhaps one last great career moment to look forward to. Trinidad and Tobago has qualified for the 2006 World Cup in Germany and will play England in the group stages. Dwight has been the team captain.

I am delighted for Dwight. I wish him and his team well. It will be quite an experience. And I'll love watching how they get on.

Although I failed to reveal the real Dwight Yorke, I still admired what he had done. I think how he made it, from his origins, is one of the more uplifting stories in football.

CHAPTER EIGHT

Football Memorabilia

I was at a Premier League club, about to see the manager. I'd arrived a little bit late, so I went straight in to what I thought was the manager's office. I found myself in a side office where a secretary was working at her desk. As I walked in, she jumped up, startled, and looked guilty. She tried to hide what she was doing from me. Naturally, I leaned forward to find out what it was.

On her desk was a line-up of gleaming, brand new footballs. In front of her, propped up, was a piece of paper with copies of all the signatures of the first-team squad. What she appeared to be doing was copying out the names of the club's stars on to a whole load of footballs. Perhaps she did this every day, who knows.

No need to name the club. OK, they play in white, which limits it, but I didn't say which season. The point is – beware. When someone, some dealer, some auction house, even some respectable charity, is offering autographed football items, it is very hard to be sure that they are genuine. Clubs want their £100,000-a-week stars to be training or resting, not tiring their wrists signing their names. Hence a bit of forgery can sometimes take place. It is understandable.

I was once on a train with the Beatles, going to Bangor in North Wales. Autograph books were being shoved through the carriage window. One kid was in tears, as he'd got three signatures, but not John's. So I signed it, John Lennon. I often look out for it at auctions.

I didn't actively collect football memorabilia until about the last ten years. By active, I mean going out to jumble sales, car boot sales and visiting fairs, dealers and specialist shops. Or even bidding at auctions. Before then, I had been a passive collector. I just built up loads of football stuff in the sense of rarely throwing away anything I had bought or come across.

I wish I'd kept that home-made football album I kept during the war, sticking in the Scottish stars. My mum threw it away. I never forgave her.

Since the 1960s, I have always kept my football programmes. That explains how I come to have in my collection my 1966 World Cup final programme. I also kept, which was most unusual at the time, the ticket stub. No one I knew had ever collected them, far less kept them in their pocket after the game was over.

I only collect paper memorabilia, which mainly means programmes, football books, magazines. I've got Spurs programmes going back to 1911 and England-Scotland programmes back to 1930. I probably won't get any further back with those two collections. The prices are now too high.

I recently paid £95 for a 1910 Everton programme. This was because of its fascinating history. Well, fascinating to me. I was writing a history of football at the time and in the book I was able to use photographs of some of the things in my own collection as illustrations.

The interesting point about this Everton programme is that it's a joint programme with Liverpool. For many years, they shared the same one. If Everton were playing at Goodison Park, it would be mainly about their first team. But it would also include information on Liverpool Reserves, who would also be playing at home that day. Next week, it would be the other way round, featuring the Liverpool first team and Everton reserves. Oh if only deadly rival clubs could be such good friends today.

Cup final programmes have always been greatly in demand, but the most desired club is Manchester United, for obvious reasons. They have the biggest fan base, followed by Chelsea, Spurs, Arsenal, Rangers and Celtic. But pre-war programmes from the smallest clubs can fetch big prices. And every British club has its collectors. The smaller the club, the fewer programmes issued.

Football programmes are the easiest football

items to collect. Most fans who go to a game buy a programme, for between £2 and £3. So it's fairly cheap to start collecting them. You won't get your money back, or anything like it, for many years to come. You can also still buy, very cheaply, ordinary programmes from the 1990s, 80s and 70s. Even 1960s programmes are still quite reasonable – just two or three pounds. The cost of the programmes from the 1950s has now begun to creep up, to around a tenner. Wartime programmes, from the 1940s, are around £20. Pre-war, then you can pay hundreds, if not thousands.

While prices have doubled in the last four or five years for good material, some items have increased in value by up to five times. For example, in 1991 at Christie's, a 1897 Cup final programme for Villa versus Everton sold for £1,600. In 2002, at Sotheby's, the same item went for £7,200.

My 1966 World Cup souvenir programme, the one I boasted about, is now worth about £50. But that ticket stub, a mere scrap of paper, is worth £150. The reason is scarcity – most people did throw them away.

Old football books, magazines, annuals,

which I also collect, have not increased in price as dramatically as programmes. And as with programmes, 1950s and 1960s publications are still relative bargains. Also excellent value are post-war and pre-war boys' 'budget books', which can be found for about £5–10. They often had attractive art work on the cover, showing a football scene, even if the contents were pretty poor.

The best produced, best written, and most fancy football books were published between around 1890 and 1910. This was when football was still being run by gents. And they were the ones reading the books. They were looking for high-quality football books to add to their sporting libraries.

Action photography didn't exist, but the studio portraits of star players and top teams were excellent. They haven't been bettered since. *Famous Footballers, 1895–96* by Alcock and Hill is the best of the photographic books, costing today about £500. Many dealers, over the years, have ruined copies by tearing out plates and selling them separately.

By the 1920s and 1930s, football had become a working-class sport. It was followed by the masses and so football publications became mass produced, printed on poor-quality paper, with less skilful writing. But they were still full of social history which is fascinating today.

Will prices continue to increase? I think so, because purchasers of football memorabilia are genuine collectors, not outsiders looking only for a profit by buying now to sell on for more money later. People collect football stuff out of love of football – and as football has become more popular, especially among the middle classes, the demand should continue to grow. That's because those middle-class collectors have a few bob to spend on daft things.

Football Memorabilia Facts
* The world record for a football shirt is £157,750 paid for Pele's 1970 World Cup final shirt.
* The record for an English shirt, as worn by Geoff Hurst in the 1966 World Cup final, is £91,750.
* The oldest known international football shirt is that worn by Arnold Kirke-Smith in the 1872 England–Scotland game. It is now on

show at the National Football Museum in Preston.

* The world record for a football programme was set in February 2005 at Sotheby's when a 1901 Spurs–Sheffield United Cup final programme went for £14,400.

* The most desirable football books are the four volumes of *Association Football and the Men who Made It* by Gibson and Pickford, 1905 – expect to pay around £500 for the set.

CHAPTER NINE

Gazza

After my experience with Dwight Yorke, I didn't want to do another football biography. So at Christmas time 2002 when I was first approached about doing Paul Gascoigne's life, I said no thanks. Gazza isn't for me.

I'd already written *The Glory Game*, about a team. I'd written *Boots, Balls and Haircuts*, about the history of football. I'd done the life of a manager, Joe Kinnear. I'd had a collection of my football articles for the *New Statesman* published, *The Fan*. I'd even done a football novel, *Striker*. This was some years ago. Funnily enough, it had been inspired by Gazza. In the novel my hero ends up in Italy, as Gazza did in real life. But in my story, he gets kidnapped and held to ransom. While locked up, he decides to write his life story.

Anyway, after all those books I had decided that's it. My football writing days were over. The publisher who rang me about Gazza was a friend who had published one of my earlier books, about Eddie Stobart. He's the man behind the lorry firm, though it would make a good name for a 1930s footballer.

Three months later, she rang me again. They had not approached any other writer, still hoping I might agree. Would I at least go and meet Gazza, and see how we got on?

I slowly began to discover the background to the project. Headline, the publisher, had bought the rights to Gazza's autobiography about five years previously. He had then been playing for Glasgow Rangers, probably earning about a million a year. He wasn't really much bothered at the time about doing his book.

Someone was going to write it, but they fell out and that never happened. Then a well-known football journalist was interested, but started preaching at Gazza about his drinking. That didn't please Gazza.

There had been various other delays over the years, for lots of reasons. It was decided it might be best to wait until he'd finished in the Premiership. Then he could say what he liked.

The publisher of course had already invested a lot of money in the project. The normal procedure for paying an author the advance is that one third is paid over when the contract is signed. One third is paid when the manuscript is completed and agreed, and the final third is paid on publication.

A big celebrity, a household name, might get up to a million pounds, paid in those stages. I don't know what Gazza got. Not as much as that, I don't think. But the publisher had paid over a large sum already – and not received a penny back in return, because the book hadn't been published yet – or even written. They were therefore keen to get Gazza matched with a writer, someone who could finally get the book out of him.

I agreed to meet Gazza at a hotel at London's Heathrow airport. He was on the way to China along with his dad and Jimmy Five Bellies, Gazza's best friend. When I arrived, they were all pretty drunk, or at least well oiled. Gazza said he was shit scared of flying. That's why he needed Dutch courage.

Because of my previous experiences, I wanted to discover three things about Gazza, before I even considered doing the book.

One, would he give me the time? Dwight was at the height of his career, so getting to see him was always difficult. But Gazza's Premiership career was now over. In theory, he would have lots of time. Apart of course from the fact that he was now going off to a remote part of China and might never be seen again. He said there would be no problems. I could have as much time with him as I wanted.

Secondly, did he really, truly want to do the book? The answer to that was yes, for pretty obvious reasons. He was in effect out of work and needed the money. The book had to be written and published for him to get the remaining two-thirds of his advance.

Would he open up? This, in a way, was my

most important question. I had been so bitterly disappointed with Dwight. Before I started working with him on that book, I had never realised his true character.

I had three hours with Gazza at that first meeting. After just an hour, I was saying, 'Paul, please, no more, no need to tell me that, that's awful, that's disgusting, listen we can never use that in a book . . .'

He is an innocent in many ways, very open, willing to tell people the most intimate, personal things.

He had never done his autobiography before – telling his story in the first person – though there had been five books written about him. So that was an extra attraction.

I had always enjoyed Gazza, the player. I watched him when he'd played for Spurs. I had suffered along with him and the whole nation when he was yellow-carded in the World Cup semi-final of 1990. I watched, amazed, at his tears.

The first problem occurred in China, after his dad and Jimmy had returned to Newcastle. He went into a series of panic attacks, binge-drinking and pill-popping.

From China, he somehow managed to get himself to Cottonwood, a clinic in Arizona, where he had been before. I feared this time he'd get himself kept in hospital and the book would be off, before I'd properly begun.

But he did return, dried out. This time he admitted he was an alcoholic, promising he would never drink again. His ex-wife Sheryl agreed to take him in for a while. Many of my early interviews took place at her lovely house in Hertfordshire, complete with swimming pool, tennis courts, big gardens.

Not everyone in Gazza's life was sure it was a good idea for him to be back with Shel, as he called her. I rather defended her. Gazza had beaten her up. She'd had a lot to suffer. She must love him, or be genuinely trying to help him recover.

It didn't last long, living with Shel. They argued a lot. And so he was on his own again.

Thanks to his friendship with Paul Ince, then at Wolves, he managed to be allowed to train at Wolves. He turned out for their reserves and moved into a hotel not far away.

For the previous five years, Gazza had not owned a house of his own. While at

Middlesbrough and Everton, he had lived in hotels or rented flats. He said he liked hotels. He also didn't mind hospitals. They seem to comfort him, protect him from real life and responsibilities.

While he was in Arizona, I had asked him to do me some notes, or tape record answers to questions I had given him.

On his return, he pulled out a massive sheet of brown paper, the sort you use for wrapping up parcels. I wondered what might be inside it. Turned out the brown paper itself was what he had brought me.

On it he had done this enormous chart of his life. It was marked 'PATH TO RECOVERY'. He had written on it all the major events in his life, personal as well as football events, from his birth in 1967 up to the age of thirty-six. Different colours and symbols indicated deaths and operations. All together, up to that time, he had had twenty-eight different operations.

It's a fascinating document, neatly done, carefully put together. Gazza is not uneducated, even if he did leave school with only two CSE levels – in English and Environmental Studies.

I came to the conclusion that Gazza's

problems were not really to do with drink. Drink was a result of his mental and emotional problems. He had used drink to escape from himself, to wipe out his bad thoughts. He is an obsessive compulsive, always wanting things in the right order. He takes most things to extremes, whether training or drinking. He's a depressive, prone to panic attacks. He's also hyperactive.

But it's not true that he suffers from attention deficit disorder, as has been alleged. He could not have filled in that enormous chart, without being able to concentrate. He could not have been first in and last out when training. He could not have been able to sit and pay attention for three hours at a time when I was interviewing him.

He did, of course, mess me around now and again, but not like Dwight did. I wasn't surprised. You come to expect that not everything will go smoothly when you are writing a book with someone. Lots of odd things can happen.

For instance, when I was doing the Beatles biography, I would make a date to see John Lennon at his big house at Weybridge, Surrey. I would arrive, as arranged, to find that John had decided it was a day for not talking.

We would swim round his swimming pool, not talking. We would watch children's afternoon TV together, not talking. Cynthia, his wife, would make us supper, which we would all eat, not talking. I could come home with an empty notebook and think bloody hell, that was a waste of time.

With Gazza, I'd arrive at his hotel in the evening and stay overnight. First thing in the morning, as he is a very early riser, partly due to the fact that he hardly sleeps, I would knock at his bedroom door.

After ten minutes or so, he would often say, 'You're doing ma fuckin' heed in.'

I would have to leave his room, walk around the hotel, have a swim, then come back later in the day.

It wasn't that he couldn't be bothered, or had something else more amusing to do, as Dwight had. It was genuinely a case of his head not being right.

He would stay in his room, playing chess with himself on his mobile phone, till he felt more able to face the world. Or at least face me.

I can be pretty exhausting when I get going.

When I finished the manuscript, I naturally sent a copy to Gazza, for him to read.

He kept promising to read it, but after six weeks, he still hadn't started. I was getting desperate as the book was about to go to the printer.

Finally, I rang him and said I'm coming up to Newcastle tomorrow morning. I'll be on the first train. I want you to have read it, so I can bring the corrected manuscript back with me.

Paul met me outside the station, looking great, with a brilliant tan – all from a sunbed. He was lean and fit with his hair newly dyed silver. Then he started moaning and groaning. He'd got up at two in the morning to start on the manuscript, managing to read for four hours, then he'd gone to the gym. He was now knackered, but had got only halfway through.

I was desperate for him to read it, every word. When he did the publicity, it would be so embarrassing if he got asked about things he knew nothing about. I hadn't made up any stories, certainly not, but I had put a few thoughts into his mouth that he hadn't actually said to me. But that is common if you are writing someone's story. Having spent so much time with Paul, I felt I knew what he was trying to say at certain moments. He just hadn't actually said the words.

Of course, what was most important was that Paul did read everything, because he might not have agreed with me. And it was his story after all.

I also wanted him to check any facts, dates or names, which I could easily have got wrong and which might hurt other people. I suspect that Roy Keane hardly read Eamon Dunphy's biography of him, not properly, judging by the way Roy smirked when being interviewed and the way he tried to avoid certain questions about what was in the book.

So I sat with Paul for another four hours while he laboriously went through every page, his head down, his brow furrowed.

'Just talk aloud the bits you don't like,' so I told him. 'I'll make notes, no need for you to write things.' But he insisted – correcting all my spelling mistakes. He did, after all, pass CSE English. He failed maths, his best subject, because his desk collapsed. All his fault. He took the screws out to see how it worked.

While he read, not stopping for food or coffee or even a break, I poked around the flat. He was staying with Jimmy Five Bellies, in his spare room. Jimmy was out working. He fixes roofs. I hadn't been to the flat before, and half expected a lads' den with fag ends, pin-ups, empty bottles, dirty clothes, dirty dishes. But it was pristine. White carpet, immaculate walls, little glass tables. In the fridge, there was no beer, only Red Bull.

After another four hours, he had finished the manuscript. He said he was about to collapse and that he could never do that again. But he insisted on driving me back to the station, which I wish he hadn't. I am always scared stiff by his driving.

On the train home, I did have a few drinks to celebrate a successful trip, and got a taxi home from King's Cross. I, too, was knackered, having got up at six to catch the early train. I went straight to bed – little knowing that I had left half of Paul's manuscript in the taxi. This was the only copy with Paul's comments and corrections marked.

About an hour later, I was wakened by loud knocking on the front door. I could hear my wife answering it, taking in some package, saying thank you. It was the taxi driver. My wife didn't know I'd left anything in the cab. Let alone something as valuable as Paul's manuscript that couldn't be replaced. So when the chap dropped off the carrier bag with it in, all my wife had in her purse was a fiver to give him to say thanks. It was worth a lot more than that.

What was amazing to me was the effort the cab driver went to. What I'd left was only the second half of the manuscript, about 200 pages, so there was no front page with my name and address on it. Or even Gazza's. It would have been understandable if the cab driver had just binned it. And I would have been distraught. I don't think Gazza could have read it again.

The taxi driver had driven halfway across London, gone up and down our street knocking at doors, as he hadn't seen which house I had gone into. All for a measly fiver. If you know any drivers of black cabs, pass on the word. I definitely owe him one. A thousand thanks, whoever it was . . .

The book turned out to be a massive success, selling over 300,000 copies in hardback and winning Sports Book of the Year. I like to think it is one of the most honest, revealing football books ever. All thanks to Gazza of course, and his willingness to expose himself.

Since the book, people are always asking me what he was really like. I say complicated, but at the same time lovely, open, friendly, generous.

While doing it, I never found anyone who had a bad word to say against him. In his drunken days, he had behaved very badly and there can be no excuse for his attacks on Shel. But for almost the last ten years, he had done no harm of any sort to anybody. So he always said.

He stayed off the booze for over two years but there have been reports recently that he's fallen off the wagon.

People often compare or link him with George Best. They think Gazza threw a brilliant career away by drink and excess. But Gazza drank for different reasons. And he didn't throw away his career.

George Best's career was over by the age of twenty-seven. People forget that Gazza, despite all his problems and endless injuries, had an excellent career. He played in the Premiership till he was thirty-five. He managed fifty-seven caps for England. He played in a World Cup semi-final.

So what will happen to him now? Well, that's the other question people ask. Who knows if he can stay off the booze.

The cynics expect him to end up bust. He has been far too generous, giving away or wasting around £10 million, including the expenses of his marriage problems. But he has managed to save some money.

I worry more about his health – physical and mental. All those operations he has had are bound to take their toll. I can see him suffering from serious arthritis as he gets older. Mentally, he is still taking medication to calm himself down, but he has become wiser, calmer with age.

So there is hope for him. He has tried a few routes to get back into the game he loves. That would be great for him if it works out. All football fans, whoever they support, must wish him well.

CHAPTER TEN

The World Cup

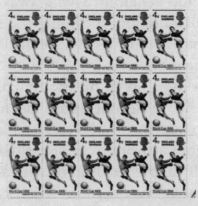

FIFA, THE GOVERNING BODY of world football, was created in 1904. It was founded by seven of the leading European countries where organised football had first begun to take off – France, Belgium, Denmark, Holland, Spain, Sweden and Switzerland.

Notice any interesting omissions? Yes. England refused to be involved. And the same goes for Scotland, Wales and Ireland. They didn't want to be mixed up with any funny foreign organisations trying to take over their game.

England's FA did eventually join in, then left, then joined again, and left again in 1928. They gave various explanations, such as disagreements about payments to amateurs, but the basic reason was a continuing feeling of natural superiority.

'I don't care a brass farthing about the improvements of the game in France, Belgium, Austria or Germany,' said Charles Sutcliffe, a member of the FA in 1928. 'The FIFA does not appeal to me. An organisation where such football associations as those of Uruguay and Paraguay, Brazil and Egypt, Bohemia and Pan Russia are co-equal with England, Scotland, Wales and Ireland, seems to me to be a case of magnifying the midgets . . .'

Goodness, how times change. When was the last time anyone considered Brazil a midget country in football terms?

The upshot was that, when FIFA organised the first World Cup in 1930, to be held in Uruguay, none of the British countries took part.

Only four European countries made the long trek to South America – France, Belgium, Romania and Yugoslavia. The King of Romania picked his national team and managed to get each player off work so they could travel abroad.

All four countries went on the same boat which took two weeks to reach Uruguay. The players exercised on deck to keep fit. On board was Jules Rimet, the French lawyer who was President of FIFA, carrying the World Cup trophy in his luggage.

Thirteen nations entered that first World Cup. Uruguay won it, beating Argentina 4–2 in the final.

England finally agreed to join FIFA after the last war, in 1946, in time to take part in the 1950 World Cup held in Brazil. They suffered the embarrassment of being beaten by the USA, 1–0, in the first round.

Since then, England's success rate in the World Cup has been pretty poor, apart of course from that glorious victory in 1966. About the nearest since then was 1990 when Gazza, almost, but not quite, helped get England into the final. And England have failed to even qualify at all – in 1974, 1978 and 1994.

Brazil, that 'midget country', leads the table with five World Cup wins, followed by Italy four, Germany three, Argentina and Uruguay twice each.

But hope springs eternally each time. When a new World Cup looms, I get carried away, over excited, thinking this could be the year, England's time has come.

I tell myself that seriously, no question, we do happen to have some really good players at present, the best batch for about thirty years – such as Rooney, Gerrard, Lampard, Terry, Joe Cole, Owen, Ferdinand, Campbell and Beckham. These are players you would expect to have a chance in any national squad. Surely they can be organised into a decent team? We'll see. Fingers crossed.

What I like about international competitions is that, on the whole, they are played fairly. You don't get a lot of stupid violence, petty gamesmanship, arguing with refs, which is so often present in normal league games.

Players know the eyes of the world are upon them. The chances are they won't be on such a world stage again. They do try hard to behave and uphold the ancient moral codes of football. For once, they do make an effort to make the beautiful game beautiful.

I also like it because you know that the players playing for Brazil or Paraguay, Egypt or Cameroon, really do come from those places. Fat chance these days of all the players turning out for Manchester United or Real Madrid actually coming from Manchester or Madrid. They are paid mercenaries, hired to go anywhere, with no loyalties.

But most of all, I like World Cups because I like football. I just want to see good football played by good players. Naturally, I want my favourite teams to win, but really, it's the football itself I love most.

When I sit at Spurs, when play is boring or not much is happening, there are always cries of 'STAND UP IF YOU HATE ARSENAL'. At Highbury, the same cry, only different, can also be heard.

There used to be a retired accountant who sat next to me in the West Stand at Spurs. Every time we heard this cry, neither of us would stand up. I would say to him, 'I'm too old to hate.' He would turn to me and say, 'I'm too old to stand up.' And we would both smile at our wit and wisdom.

During these last fifty years, I haven't lost the excitement of going to a game, any game. I might moan and groan about getting there, about the parking and the awful traffic. I might groan and gasp as I drag myself up the concrete steps, push my way down ugly, smelly corridors, and shove myself through the masses stuffing their faces with burgers and beer. But then, at last, I get my first glimpse of the gleaming green grass. My heart does give a little leap of anticipation.

Within half an hour I know I will be groaning at some useless player, or telling the ref he is a self-abuser. Nonetheless I will be sitting there hoping for a little moment of magic, a sequence of inspired passes, an individual piece of football genius, something that will lift me out of my seat.

While I love being there, in the flesh, I also enjoy every live game of football on TV. These days, that means almost every night and twice on Saturdays and Sundays. I see it as the pudding, the treat at the end of my working day.

I love the fact that football is international.

You can go anywhere in the world, without a word of the local language, watch a game and know what's going on. You can make yourself understood, just by talking football talk.

The chances are you will know some of their star names, just as they will know about some of yours. Thanks to TV, world-class players really are world-class, known worldwide.

I remember in 1968, when I happened to be living in Malta, I was furious that I was going to be missing Manchester United in their European final and that locally no one would be interested. Then weeks before the game, I began to notice that on buses and in taxis, the drivers were hanging little Madonna-like images of Bobby Charlton and George Best beside their real Madonnas.

I like to think, at every game, that I am communing with all football fans, all over the world. At the same moment, they will be going through much the same rituals as I am.

I also like to imagine, and this is a bit potty, that I am in touch with all the dead football fans – football followers, from all over the world, who have gone before, during these last 150 years.

I feel quite envious, in a way, of all those young fans, the ones who will live on after me. They'll be able to see all those wonderful games to come which I will miss. Curses.

But I tell myself I will still be there. In spirit. A love of football lives for ever . . .

WORLD BOOK DAY

Quick Reads

Quick Reads are published alongside and in partnership with BBC RaW.

We would like to thank all our partners in the *Quick* Reads project for all their help and support:

Department for Education and Skills
Trades Union Congress
The Vital Link
The Reading Agency
National Literacy Trust

Quick Reads would also like to thank the Arts Council England and National Book Tokens for their sponsorship.

We would also like to thank the following companies for providing their services free of charge: SX Composing for typesetting all the titles; Icon Reproduction for text reproduction; Norske Skog, Stora Enso, PMS and Iggusend for paper/board supplies; Mackays of Chatham, Cox and Wyman, Bookmarque, White Quill Press, Concise, Norhaven and GGP for the printing.

www.worldbookday.com